Elizabeth of Glamis

ELIZABETH
OF GLAMIS

*An illustrated life
of the Queen Mother*

First published in 1990
by Canongate Publishing Limited,
Edinburgh

British Library Cataloguing in Publication Data
Wolsey, Terry
Elizabeth of Glamis
1. Great Britain. Elizabeth, Queen, consort of George VI,
I. Title
941084092

ISBN 0 –86241–329–X

Text Terry Wolsey
Illustrations

Design by Caleb Rutherford
Set in Bembo by Falcon Typographic Art Ltd.
Printed and bound by Butler & Tanner, Frome, Somerset

Title page

*The Strathmore family in the Drawing Room
at Glamis Castle. Elizabeth and David are in
the foreground building a house of cards.*

CONTENTS

A Little Princess   *1*

The Great War   *13*

A Royal Romance   *23*

The Smiling Duchess   *37*

Edward and Mrs Simpson   *51*

Queen Consort   *57*

World War II   *63*

Peace at Last   *81*

Queen Mother   *91*

PHOTOGRAPH ACKNOWLEDGEMENTS

The Publishers gratefully acknowledge permission granted from the following sources
for the right to reproduce photographs in *Elizabeth of Glamis*:

D.C. Thomson Ltd, *black and white: p.2, p.4, p.7 top, p.10 top, p.11 top, p.11 below,
p.12 top, p.15, p.16, p.21 below, p.27 top, p.28 below, p.29, p.30 top, centre, below, p.33
top, p.35, p.39 top right, below, p.41 top, below, p.42, p.43 left and right, p.46 top, below,
p.48 top, centre, below, p.49 top left, right, p.51, p.53 below, p.54 top, p.55 top, p.56, p.59
above, p.63, p.66 top, below, p.67, p.68, p.70, p.71, p.72, top, below, p.73 top, p.75 top left,
below, p.78, p.79 below, p.80, p.83 top, p.84 top, below, p.86, p.87 top, p.92, p.93 below,
p.94 below, p.100 centre, p.101 top, p.105 top; colour: p.102 centre, p.109 below.* **Mary,
Countess of Strathmore**, *black and white: p.1, p.3, p.5 top, below, p.6 top, below, p.7
below, p.8, p.9, p.12 below, p.17 top, centre, below, p.18, p.19 top, centre, below, p.20, p.21
top, p.22, p.24 below, p.25, p.26 below, p.27 below, p.28 top, p.32, p.40; colour: p.103
top.* **Aberdeen Journals Ltd**, *black and white: p.13, p.35 top, below, p.37, p.38, p.39 top
left, p.45 top, p.47, p.49 below, p.52, p.53 top, p.57, p.60, p.61 top right, p.62 below, p.69,
p.74 top, below, p.76 below, p.79 top, p.94 top, p.95, p.100 top, p.101 below, p.106 top.*
Popperfoto, *black and white: p.33 below, p.58 left, p.58-59, p.59 below right, p.61 top left,
below, p.65, p.81, p.82-83 below, p.87 below, p.88 top, below, p.89, p.90.* **J MacDonald,
Wick**, *black and white: p.96 below, p.99 top. colour: p.96 below, p.97 top, below, p.98, p.99
below.* **Illustrated London News**, *black and white: p.14, p.23 left and right, p.26 top, p.54
below, p.55 below.* **Syndication International**, *black and white: p.44 top, below. colour:
p.104 below, p.107, p.109 top.* **The Daily Record**, *colour: p.99 below, p.102 top, p.108
below, p.110 below.* **Times Newspapers**, *black and white: p.34.* **George Outram Ltd**,
black and white: p.10 below, p.50, p.72 centre, p.75 top right. **The Press Association**,
black and white: p.85, p.93 top. colour: p.102 below, p.103 below. **Camera Press**, *colour:
p.104 top, p.106 below, p.110 top.* **Scotsman Publications Ltd.**, *black and white: p.31
top, p.62 top, p.105 below.* **Hulton Picture Library**, *black and white: p.31 below, p.77.*
Imperial War Museum, *black and white: p.73 below, p.76 top.* **Tim Graham**, *colour:
p.108 top.* **John Paul, Inverness**, *black and white p.96 top.* **Michael Plomer/Octopus
Group**, *colour: p.100 below.*

AUTHOR'S NOTE

A book of this nature is never the product of one person only, and I am indebted to many people for their assistance. I would particularly like to thank the following people: Mary, Countess of Strathmore, for her tremendous enthusiasm, help and advice throughout; Neville Moir, for trusting his judgement; Graham Mitchell for his excellent photographic services; Irene Wolsey for her informed opinion on the 'War Years'; Tom Forsyth at Aberdeen Journals, and Douglas Spence and the ladies at D.C. Thomson, for their superb assistance with photographs; Fiona Morrison for her positive criticism and advice; and finally Evelyn Sim for typing the manuscript and 'saving the day'. My sincere thanks to you all.

Terry Wolsey

April 1990

May the owner, of this book be

Hung, Drawn, & Quartered.

- - - - - - - - - -

"Yes"

Hung in Diamonds, Drawn in a Coach & Four,
And, Quartered in the Best House, in the
Land.

March 12th 1917

W. H. Harrop
8th Seaforth's.

FOREWORD

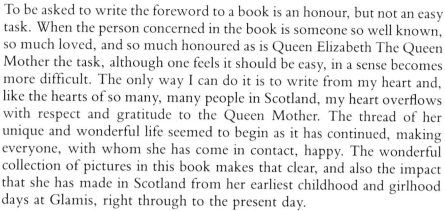

To be asked to write the foreword to a book is an honour, but not an easy task. When the person concerned in the book is someone so well known, so much loved, and so much honoured as is Queen Elizabeth The Queen Mother the task, although one feels it should be easy, in a sense becomes more difficult. The only way I can do it is to write from my heart and, like the hearts of so many, many people in Scotland, my heart overflows with respect and gratitude to the Queen Mother. The thread of her unique and wonderful life seemed to begin as it has continued, making everyone, with whom she has come in contact, happy. The wonderful collection of pictures in this book makes that clear, and also the impact that she has made in Scotland from her earliest childhood and girlhood days at Glamis, right through to the present day.

I suppose the first people to fall under the Queen Mother's spell, apart from her own immediate family and people who had known her from childhood, were the soldiers who came to Glamis to be nursed back to health during the 1914–18 war, when Glamis castle became a convalescent hospital for war wounded. One of the young soldiers wrote the following, most strangely prophetic words in the then seventeen-year-old Lady Elizabeth Bowes Lyon's autograph book. 'May you be hung, drawn and quartered. Yes, hung in diamonds, drawn in a coach and four, and quartered in the best house in the land'. Surely a measure of the great admiration and affection felt for young Lady Elizabeth by the soldiers for whom she did so much to restore back to health and happiness.

After her marriage to the Duke of York in 1923 the whole of the United Kingdom took her to their hearts, but it is to Scotland that she has returned, whenever possible, all through her life. Her own two much loved homes, the Castle of Mey in Caithness, and Birkhall in Aberdeenshire, hold a very special place in her heart and the people of Scotland know what a real love and understanding she has for Scotland and its people. Her great love for and interest in Glamis, her vivid and happy memories of her early life here and her encouragement to us, have been a source of great strength and inspiration to me and my family. It is a support for which I shall never cease to be grateful, and I feel sure that many people who read this book will share my gratitude for the love, service and example that the Queen Mother has given to Scotland throughout her life.

Mary Strathmore

Glamis Castle
Angus
Scotland

March 1990

A Little Princess

Elizabeth on the steps of the family home at St Paul's Walden Bury, aged two.

On Saturday, August 4th, 1900, a very special baby was born into the large Victorian family of Lord and Lady Glamis. Delighted, if perhaps a little surprised by their late addition to the family, they christened their ninth child Elizabeth Angela Marguerite. Although a happy event for the Bowes Lyon family the birth was not heralded in the newspapers or celebrated in public. The place of birth was London, and the christening took place seven weeks later at St Paul's Walden Bury, the family home in Hertfordshire. Family and friends gathered at St Paul's on September 23rd, 1900, to celebrate the new arrival and to wish her a long and happy life. No-one would have dreamt then that the baby Elizabeth, fourth daughter to Lord and Lady Glamis, would one day marry Albert, Duke of York, and later become his Queen Consort.

Her father, Claude Bowes Lyon, was the oldest son of a family of eleven, and grandson to the 12th Earl of Strathmore and Kinghorne, an old and highly respected Scots title. He was especially close to his paternal grandmother, Charlotte Grimstead, who left him St Paul's Walden Bury in her will when she died in 1881. An officer in the 2nd Life Guards, Claude Bowes Lyon was courting Nina Cecilia Cavendish Bentinck at the time, the eighteen year old daughter of The Reverend The Honourable C.W.F. Bentinck and Mrs Bentinck. Cecilia's father had died when she was only three and so her cousin, the 6th Duke of Portland, gave her away at her wedding in July 1881. Cecilia's great-grandfather was the 3rd Duke of Portland, who was Prime

Minister twice; in 1783 and 1807-9. Had she been a son Cecilia would have inherited the title from her uncle, the 5th Duke of Portland. Claude resigned his commission with the Life Guards and they commenced their lives together in the rambling red brick Queen Anne mansion of St Paul's Walden Bury.

The Bowes Lyon family was a large and happy one. Elizabeth's oldest sister, Mary Frances, known as May, was seventeen years her senior. Then followed brothers Patrick, John, Alexander and Fergus. Another sister, Rose Constance, was ten years older, and next to Elizabeth was Michael, who was seven years her senior. At the age of two Elizabeth

The Bowes Lyon family at St Paul's Walden Bury, 1903. Elizabeth was the ninth of ten children born to Lord and Lady Glamis. Sadly, their eldest daughter, Violet Hyacinth, died at the age of eleven before Elizabeth was born. Here, Elizabeth is standing next to her mother and her younger brother, David, is sitting on Lady Glamis' knee.

was joined by a younger brother, David, and the family was complete.
Violet Hyacinth, Lord and Lady Glamis' first born, died tragically of
diphtheria at the age of eleven, only seventeen days after Michael's birth.
Consequently Elizabeth and David never knew their oldest sister. Lady
Strathmore was the keystone of the family, admired and adored by all.
One of her daughters recalled: 'Mother was a very wonderful woman,
very talented , very go-ahead and so upright. She had a terrific sympathy:
the young used to pour their troubles out to her and ask her for advice,
often when they would not go to their own parents. She was extremely
artistic. She sewed lovely embroidery, which she designed herself. She
had an extremely good ear for music, she would go to a concert and
listen to the music, and come back and play it perfectly.'

In the days without radio or television the family would create their
own entertainment, gathering around the piano after dinner and singing
the popular songs of the day.

Clara Knight joined the Bowes Lyon staff as nanny to Elizabeth
shortly after the birth. As Clara was a little difficult for Elizabeth to
pronounce she called her 'Allah', and the name affectionately stuck. Allah
described the young Elizabeth as 'an exceptionally happy, easy baby,
crawling early, running at thirteen months and speaking very young.'
As the youngest Bowes Lyons David and Elizabeth were inseparable
and played together like twins. Both children were especially close to
their mother, who said that her new family made her feel quite young
again. According to Mary Frances, later Lady Elphinstone, she was not
as strict with her youngest as she had been with her first born. She
referred to her two most indulged offspring as 'my two Benjamins' and
confessed that she was, on occasion, mistaken for their grandmother.
Elizabeth had a special relationship with her mother. Lady Elphinstone

4

Elizabeth in the wood at St Paul's Walden Bury.

recalled, 'As Elizabeth was the youngest daughter she was very much with our mother . . . My father adored her too, but it was really my mother who brought her up.'

Elizabeth greatly impressed Katherine, Duchess of Atholl, when she visited Lady Glamis in London in 1903. The Duchess recalled that she 'was very impressed by the charm and dignity of a little daughter, two or three years old, who came into the room . . . as if a little Princess had stepped out of an eighteenth century picture.'

With the older children away at boarding school David and Elizabeth had the run of the house and garden. In later years Her Majesty described the wood at St Paul's to her biographer Cynthia Asquith:

> At the bottom of the garden is THE WOOD - the haunt of fairies, with its anemones and ponds and moss grown statues, and the big oak under which she reads and where the two ring doves contentedly coo . . . There are carpets of primroses to sit on and her small brother David is always with her.

One of the Queen Mother's earliest memories is a visit to Glamis Castle in 1903, the occasion being her grandparents' golden wedding

5

celebrations. The following year the 13th Earl died and his titles were passed to Claude Bowes Lyon who, at the age of forty-nine, became the 14th Earl of Strathmore and Kinghorne, with an inheritance which included the Strathmore homes of Glamis Castle in Angus and Streatlam Castle in County Durham. Elizabeth and her sisters were now Lady Elizabeth, Lady Mary and Lady Rose, whilst her brothers acquired the title 'The Honourable . . . '.

Although considered a commoner when she married the Duke of York in 1923, the Queen Mother possesses her fair share of Royal Blood. She is directly descended from King Robert the Bruce; whose great granddaughter Jean married Sir John Lyon in 1377, when the

Lyon dynasty was created. Four centuries later the Lyons married into the powerful and immensely wealthy Bowes family of Streatlam, County Durham, and the Queen Mother's grandfather, the 13th Earl of Strathmore, assumed the present name of Bowes Lyon. Elizabeth was known to drop the Bowes on occasion, preferring to introduce herself as 'Elizabeth Lyon'.

Home was still, for most of the year, St Paul's Walden Bury, but the family now travelled north every August to spend the holiday at the family seat of Glamis Castle. The whole household would uproot and travel to Scotland. Silver, china, clothes and toys were all packed away in great trunks and everyone and everything boarded the Flying Scotsman for the exciting journey north.

Glamis was a magical place for Elizabeth and David; the secret rooms, passageways and ghosts providing perfect material for their fertile imaginations. It was not unknown for two small creatures draped in sheets to appear before older members of the family, emulating the 'Grey Lady' of Glamis. There was great mirth when the pair poured 'boiling oil' from the castle ramparts. Although only water, it was no doubt an unwelcome surprise to the visitor below. Elizabeth and David were fond of playing tennis and Elizabeth enjoyed riding an old donkey in the

'Everything we did together was fun.' Sir David Bowes Lyon.

In the Italian Garden at Glamis. Both David and Elizabeth acquired a love of gardens from their mother, the Countess of Strathmore, who designed the Italian Garden.

castle grounds, her beloved pony 'Bobs' remaining in Hertfordshire. The children loved to play in the Italian Garden, designed by their mother, who was a gifted gardener. Both David and Elizabeth learnt to share Lady Strathmore's passion for gardening; later Sir David Bowes Lyon studied at Kew Gardens and Her Majesty designed the gardens at her home in Caithness, the Castle of Mey.

Elizabeth's father , a quiet, upright gentleman, and now Earl of Strathmore had also become Lord Lieutenant of Forfarshire, a duty he took most seriously. It was he who impressed upon Elizabeth the importance of service to the community. Born into a privileged family, Elizabeth was taught that with privilege comes certain obligations. Her Majesty's unstinting service and duty to her country demonstrates that her father taught her well.

Lord Strathmore encouraged all his sons to play cricket and the castle team regularly played against local teams. Michael Bowes Lyon remembered the matches with affection. 'I always loved the cricket up there. I shall always remember Jock opening the bowling, later on relieved by Plowright and my father, very round arm. The special umpire, Mr Arthur Fossett, short, round, red faced and fat, was perfectly trained never to no-ball father and always give his appeals out.' The matches were never too serious and always intended to be fun. When Lord Strathmore achieved a hat trick of three wickets in three balls against the Dundee Drapers his team celebrated by buying him a new Panama hat.

Lord Strathmore, in Panama hat, is accompanied by Elizabeth on the cricket pitch at Glamis.

Elizabeth loved dressing up.

'Lady Elizabeth was adorable,' said her governess, Laurel Grey.

There were strawberries and cream teas on the lawn at Lady Strathmore's garden parties, to which the local people of Forfar and Kirriemuir were invited. The Castle was always full of guests and Elizabeth was taught from a young age to entertain and look after the visitors. It was considered Elizabeth's duty to show them to their rooms and make them feel welcome. Many distinguished visitors came to stay, and Elizabeth is said to have charmed them all. Lady Scott, wife of the explorer, described Glamis as 'a glorious place. Little Lady Elizabeth Lyon showed me over.' The Strathmore piper played at dinner each evening. Today the Queen Mother has a great fondness for the pipes; she enjoys listening to their distinctive sound, even at close quarters.

Elizabeth was indulged by all the family and they referred to her fondly as 'Princess'. Lady Strathmore had a brocade dress made specially for her in the style of Elizabeth I, a copy from a Van Dyck painting. As a child the Queen Mother loved dressing up. In conversation with Cynthia Asquith she recalled that at Glamis there was 'a wonderful chest full of period costumes and the wigs that went with their gorgeousness.' In 1908 the book *Princes and Princesses* by Leonora Lang was specially dedicated to her. The final chapter was titled *The Troubles of Princess Elizabeth* and opened with the question, 'What reign in English History do you best like to read about? Oh, Queen Elizabeth, of course!'

Elizabeth was taught at home, like most of the girls of her day. David joined her for lessons until the age of ten, when he left for prep school. According to one of their governesses, Miss Laurel Gray, Elizabeth was 'adorable'. Lady Strathmore asked Miss Gray to keep an account book of the children's progress. 'When they were good, a good mark and a penny. And of course a bad mark, that was shocking. Elizabeth wasn't

too good but she always had a good mark, she was naturally a good scholar. A bad mark made no difference to David. I was as strict as I could be, he was terrible!'

Elizabeth and David learnt to speak fluent French from their Governess Mlle Lang, and they both received dance instruction at Glamis from a Mr Neill of Forfar. Mr Neill would play the fiddle and jig energetically whilst the two youngest Bowes Lyons performed their steps. On one occasion in 1909 Lady Strathmore arranged a surprise concert for visitors to Glamis. Elizabeth, wearing her 'Van Dyck' dress, and David, dressed as a jester in the Strathmore colours, danced for the guests, accompanied by Mr Neill on fiddle and Lady Strathmore at the piano. Miss Gray remembered 'Elizabeth loved dressing up.' And of her dress, 'she was very pretty in it'. A guest at Lady Strathmore's tea party was the local minister, the Rev. John Stirton. Mr Stirton enquired of Elizabeth whom she was meant to be. 'I call myself Princess Elizabeth,' came the reply.

On November 21st, 1908, Patrick, Lord Glamis, married Lady Dorothy Osborne at the chapel at Wellington Barracks. Elizabeth was the youngest bridesmaid and David was a page. As well as the traditional guard of honour the newlyweds were greeted by the Strathmore pipers in full Highland dress. The following July Mary Frances married the 16th Baron Elphinstone at St Margaret's, Westminster, and Elizabeth and David were in attendance. Elizabeth, as one of the bridesmaids, wore a white Romney gown with a blue sash and a large picture hat, and carried a fan instead of flowers. David was resplendent in a kilt of Lyon tartan. The older brothers and sisters were leaving the family to begin their own, and so the two youngest Bowes Lyons became closer than ever.

'We were never separated if we could avoid it.'
Sir David Bowes Lyon.

David and Elizabeth dressing up again. He wears a jester's outfit in the Strathmore colours. The family was the last in Scotland to retain a jester.

In 1911 Elizabeth and David visited their maternal grandmother, the twice widowed Mrs Harry Warren Scott, at her villa outside Florence, the Villa Caponi. They were accompanied by their Aunt Violet, Mrs Scott's unmarried daughter, with whom they travelled to Florence aboard the Rome Express. Violet took them to visit the Uffizi and Pitti Palaces, and later they ventured as far as Venice. They made several happy journeys to Italy prior to the first World War. The Strathmores also had a home in Italy, at Bordighera on the Riviera coast. It was this that inspired Lady Strathmore to create the Italian Garden at Glamis, and there that Lord Strathmore spent much of his time after the death of his wife.

The Coronation of King George V and Queen Mary took place on June 22nd, 1911. Lord and Lady Strathmore, dressed in their ceremonial robes, took their places at Westminster, whilst Elizabeth and David watched the carriage processions from the house of a family friend. Elizabeth would have seen Prince Albert pass by in an open carriage with no idea that she was cheering her future husband.

Later that year tragedy struck the family. On October 19th the men were out shooting on the Glamis estate, accompanied by the ladies with their picnic baskets. Alexander, Lord and Lady Strathmore's third son, elected to stay behind as he had been feeling unwell. He retired to bed and died in his sleep at the age of twenty four. The whole family was shocked, but Elizabeth and David were grief stricken.

The following year, 1912, David left for his prep school at Broadstairs on the Kent coast. Elizabeth missed him 'horribly' and couldn't wait for the holidays when they could play together again. Theirs was a special closeness. Later Sir David said, 'We were never separated if we could avoid it . . . everything we did together was fun.' Elizabeth and Rose were the only two children now remaining at home, and they grew even closer to their mother who, still in mourning for the death of her son, appreciated her daughters' help in running the household.

Elizabeth missed David terribly when he left for prep school.

12

The Great War

Since the autumn of 1912, war had been rampaging through Europe and it was only a matter of time before Britain was inevitably forced to join in. On August 4th, 1914, as the Lady Elizabeth looked forward to a visit to The London Coliseum to celebrate her fourteenth birthday, King George V was holding urgent talks with his advisors. Elizabeth was a keen theatre goer; she particularly enjoyed the plays of J. M. Barrie, 'Thrums'(Kirriemuir) being only a few miles from Glamis. On this occasion she was going to see a vaudeville programme with Charles Hawtrey and G. P. Huntly; a box had been reserved at the theatre for her party. On the way there the streets of London were thronged with people waving Union Jacks, the King having issued an ultimatum to Germany. The Russian ballerina Fedorowa, who was performing that evening, was greeted with rousing cheers; the Russians, after all, were our allies. By the time that Elizabeth returned home to 20 St James' Square, Britain was at war with Germany. King George V recorded in his diary, ' . . . I held a council meeting at 10.45 to declare war with Germany, it is a terrible catastrophe but it is not our fault.'

Elizabeth attends the Glamis village fête in 1915. She helped as a stall holder at a charity sale in aid of The Red Cross.

*During the Great War Glamis Castle was converted into a Red Cross hospital for convalescent soldiers.
Over fifteen hundred service men were cared for by Lady Strathmore, Elizabeth and her older sister Rose.
Elizabeth and Lady Strathmore are seen here, with some of the wounded, in the castle forecourt.*

Elizabeth's brothers lost no time in joining up and were soon serving with their regiments; Patrick, Jock and Fergus with the Black Watch, and Michael with the Royal Scots. Throughout the land young men were marrying their sweethearts, and it was no different with the Bowes Lyon family. Fergus married Lady Christian Dawson-Damer on September 17th at Buxted in Sussex, and the family then rushed north to Scotland for Jock's marriage to Fenella Hepburn-Stuart-Forbes-Trefusis a week later.

Immediately after the wedding Elizabeth travelled with her mother and sister Rose to Glamis, where the Castle was being converted for hospital use. Red Cross volunteers helped them to move beds into the dining room and billiard room in readiness for the wounded. Lady Strathmore insisted that as little furniture be moved as possible, so as to create a homely atmosphere for the men. Later the Queen Mother told her biographer, Cynthia Asquith,

> During these first few months we were so busy knitting, knitting, knitting and making shirts for the local battalion, the 5th Black Watch. My chief occupation was crumpling up tissue paper until it was so soft that it no longer crackled, to put into the linings of sleeping bags. Lessons were quite neglected.

Although too young to train formally as a nurse at the time, Elizabeth busied herself running errands for the men, collecting their tobacco from the village shop and writing their letters for them.

The first convalescents arrived from Dundee Royal Infirmary in December 1914. Rose was in London training to be a nurse, so it was up to Elizabeth to make the soldiers feel welcome and comfortable. Too young to train formally as a nurse herself, Elizabeth kept busy running errands for the men, taking them on tours of the Castle, and writing letters to their families. There was even time for the occasional game of billiards with the more able patients. Rose returned duly qualified as the first of the badly maimed convalescents arrived at Glamis. These men had seen the full horror of the trenches and were shattered both in body and in spirit. Elizabeth saw to it that they were never short of tobacco and cigarettes and her kind words and willing smile did much to alleviate their distress.

In September 1915 Fergus returned home to Glamis to spend his first wedding anniversary with his wife and baby daughter. He returned to the Front only to be killed in action at the battle of Loos in France the day after his return. His death shocked the whole family but the Countess in particular found it hard to bear and for a time Elizabeth took her mother's place in running the Castle. In May 1916 Elizabeth was a bridesmaid to her sister Rose when she married William Spencer Leveson Gower at the church of St James, Piccadilly. She returned to Glamis with her mother and took on many of the responsibilities that had previously belonged to Rose.

Soldiers in the dining room at Glamis.

Elizabeth, seated with two nurses, at Glamis.

The convalescents sit outside on a summer's day.

In September 1916 the keep at Glamis caught fire, and the blaze quickly spread to the castle. Disaster was averted when Elizabeth called the Dundee Fire Brigade, then set about dousing the flames with jugs of water, assisted by David, and Lady Strathmore. Damage to the Castle was minimal, but the keep was completely destroyed.

In September of the same year Elizabeth and David had to act quickly to save Glamis from destruction. Most of the soldiers were on an outing to the cinema when Elizabeth noticed smoke rising from the keep. She telephoned for help from the Dundee and Forfar fire brigades as well as the local Glamis station. She and David then set about organising everyone into a chain, passing buckets and jugs of water. When a water tank burst they managed to divert the water from the drawing room, and quickly commenced the removal of furniture and pictures under threat. Their brave efforts undoubtedly saved the castle from ruin.

Above and left: Members of the Dundee Fire Brigade douse the flames, assisted by Elizabeth, David and Lady Strathmore.

Below: The charred remains of the keep roof.

Every morning Elizabeth went to the chapel at Glamis with her mother for morning worship, and often they were joined by the convalescent soldiers. In November 1916 Elizabeth's confirmation was due, but instead of a private ceremony at the Glamis chapel she chose to be confirmed with the young girls of Forfar at St John's Episcopal Church. Margaret Cadenhead was confirmed with the Queen Mother at St John's. She recalls that 'We were having our veils put on and I think I must have come against something. So she (Lady Elizabeth) said my veil had gone a bit askew and said "I hope mine's all right."' Both girls were dressed in white with veils. 'She had her hair tied back with a bow. Lovely hair and lovely eyes, beautiful blue eyes. She was just like one of ourselves, very sweet.' Mrs Cadenhead also met the Lady Elizabeth at the Castle when she took part in a tableau to entertain the soldiers. 'The soldiers all seemed to be charmed with her and said that she brightened up their day with her smile and chatter. She kept the soldiers cheery with her patter and smiles. They all liked her very, very much.'

Many of the soldiers were Australians and New Zealanders and Lady Elizabeth was to meet some of them again in years to come when touring Australasia as the Duchess of York and as Queen Mother.

In 1917 more bad news came as a War Office telegram arrived announcing Michael's death at the Front. David, however, insisted that this could not be so. He had seen Michael in a dream with a bandaged head, and was convinced he was still alive. This was of little consolation to the rest of the family at the time, but David's prophecy proved to be correct. Three months later Elizabeth's last letter was acknowledged. Michael had been shot through the head and had been too ill to write. He was a prisoner of war in Germany, where he remained until his release in 1919.

Although the war ended in November 1918 Glamis Castle remained a Red Cross Hospital throughout the next year, by which time some fifteen hundred servicemen had passed through Glamis Castle. Elizabeth got to know each and every one of them and maintained a correspondence with many of them for years to come. These men had sacrificed their innocence on the battlefields of Flanders, Ypres and Loos, and Elizabeth, in turn, sacrificed some of her youth and natural gaiety in caring for them. Her formative teenage years had been spent entirely at Glamis throughout the duration of the war. By its close she demonstrated a maturity that belied her eighteen years.

Elizabeth seated between David and a soldier at Glamis.

Elizabeth and Rose welcome a wounded soldier to Glamis.

'She makes every man feel chivalrous and gallant towards her,'   Sir Henry 'Chips' Channon.

A Royal Romance

Elizabeth, seated at the wheel of the family car.

Previous page: Lady Elizabeth first met Prince Albert at a party given by Lady Leicester in 1906.

As the last soldiers left Glamis, Elizabeth returned to the family home in St James Square, London. The war over, it was time for light hearted fun. Elizabeth joined in the round of parties, dances and outings and soon had a host of admirers. However she was never part of the cigarette smoking 'fast' set that the Prince of Wales frequented, preferring to mix with her own friends and family. Mabell, Countess of Airlie, a neighbour at Cortachy and Lady in Waiting to Queen Mary commented, 'her radiant vitality and a blending of gaiety, kindness and sincerity made her irresistible to men.' Her dancing was so admired that she acquired the accolade of 'best dancer in London'.

Elizabeth relaxes with with two friends at Glamis.

24

A keen Girl Guide, in 1920 she became District Commissioner for Glamis and was very proud when Princess Mary (with whom she shared her enthusiasm) came to inspect 'her' Girl Guides. It is popularly considered that Elizabeth first came to the attention of Prince Albert through her friendship with Princess Mary; however as a long established family (the Strathmores are one of the ten oldest peerages in Scotland) Elizabeth had mixed with the Royal Family from childhood. The Earl of Strathmore recalled, 'They first met, so far as I can remember, at a children's tea party, when Lady Elizabeth was a little girl of five or six. The party was given by Lady Leicester, the Prince was then a schoolboy. They have been friendly ever since, and have met frequently in town and country.'

In May 1920 both Elizabeth and 'Bertie', as the Prince was affectionately known, attended a ball held by Lord and Lady Farquhar in Grosvenor Square. Bertie informed the Countess of Airlie that he had fallen in love that evening, 'although he did not realise it until later.' Bertie became a regular visitor at St Paul's and in the autumn of 1920 he was invited to shoot at Glamis. He enjoyed the relaxed atmosphere

Out shooting on the moors at Glamis. The Duke of York and the Prince of Wales, both friends of Elizabeth's brothers, were invited to shoot at Glamis. They are seen here with Elizabeth, Rose and Lord Strathmore.

The Duke of York was invited to shoot at Glamis in 1920.

that prevailed in the Strathmore household, so different from his own formal upbringing, and he was totally enchanted with Elizabeth. Queen Mary commented to Lady Airlie, 'I have discovered that he (Bertie) is very much attracted to Lady Elizabeth Bowes Lyon. He's always talking about her. She seems a charming girl but I don't know her very well.' Lady Airlie replied, 'I had known her all her life, and could say nothing but good of her.'

By the spring of next year Bertie consulted his father. 'You'll be a lucky fellow if she accepts you.' Bertie proposed, and Elizabeth refused him. Perhaps Elizabeth felt that the responsibility of Royalty was too heavy to bear. After all, the war was just ended, and she was still only twenty. Or perhaps she was not yet in love. Only Her Majesty knows the real reasons why she decided against accepting Bertie.

A pensive Elizabeth at Bisham Abbey.

The Duke was devastated. The Countess of Strathmore, who had grown fond of Bertie, wrote in her diary, 'I do hope he will find a nice wife who will make him happy. I like him so much and he is a man who will be made or marred by his wife.' Queen Mary too was disappointed, recording that Elizabeth was 'the only girl who could make Bertie happy.' Elizabeth and Bertie continued to meet, however, and Bertie was again invited to Glamis. The couple played tennis together in the Castle grounds; the Duke was an excellent left handed player, having won the RAF Doubles competition in 1920 with his friend Wing Commander Louis Greig at Wimbledon.

Bertie loved to visit Elizabeth at Glamis where the atmosphere was always relaxed and friendly.

Tennis was a favourite pastime at Glamis.

During the autumn of 1921 Queen Mary visited Glamis with her daughter Princess Mary and Mabell, the Countess of Airlie. Lady Strathmore was ill at the time and so Elizabeth acted as hostess to the Royal party. Queen Mary came to see for herself, and was impressed. In February 1922 Princess Mary married Viscount Lascelles, and Elizabeth was one of her bridesmaids. Bertie returned to Glamis the following autumn. 'The more I see of her, the more I like her', he wrote to Queen Mary.

Queen Mary, accompanied by her daughter Princess Mary, visited Glamis in 1921. The party is seen seated in the Italian Garden.

With the Earl of Strathmore at Glamis, 1922.

On January 5th, 1923 the *Daily News* incorrectly reported: 'A Scottish Bride for the Prince of Wales . . . . An Official Announcement Imminent.' Bertie was furious, and the Prince of Wales issued a denial. 'A few days ago the *Daily News* announced the forthcoming engagement of the Prince of Wales to an Italian Princess. Today the same journal states on what is claimed to be unquestionable authority that the formal announcement of His Royal Highness's engagement to a daughter of a Scottish Peer will be made within the next two or three months. We are officially authorised to say that this report is as devoid of foundation as was the previous . . .'

On January 13th Elizabeth and Bertie took a walk through the wood at St Paul's where Elizabeth had spent so many happy days playing as a child. Bertie proposed in person and was accepted. His telegram to Sandringham read 'All right Bertie'; he was engaged to his 'darling Elizabeth'. On January 15th the Court Circular published the following

Their engagement was announced in The Times *Court Circular of 16th January, 1923:*

It is with greatest pleasure that the King and Queen announce the betrothal of their beloved son the Duke of York to the Lady Elizabeth Bowes Lyon, daughter of the Earl and Countess of Strathmore, to which union the King has gladly given his consent.

announcement: 'It is with the greatest pleasure that the King and Queen announce the betrothal of their beloved son the Duke of York to the Lady Elizabeth Bowes Lyon, daughter of the Earl and Countess of Strathmore, to which union the King has gladly given his consent.'

Upon reading the announcement Sir Henry Channon wrote in his diary: 'I was so startled and almost fell out of bed when I read the Court Circular. We have all hoped, waited, so long for this romance to prosper, that we had begun to despair that she would ever accept him . . . He is the luckiest of men, and there's not a man in England today who doesn't envy him. The clubs are in gloom.'

Bertie wished Elizabeth to choose her own engagement ring; Elizabeth chose the stones and design, and the ring was made specially for her; a sapphire accompanied by two diamonds. Elizabeth's Girl Guides were terribly excited by the engagement, and Elizabeth paid a special visit to the Girl Guide hut on the Glamis estate to show the Guides her ring. Miss Janet Fox, a member of the troop, later in service at the Castle, remembered, 'She came up one day when we had our meeting to show us her engagement ring, and everybody of course was delighted. A beautiful ring that she had on—sapphire. We used to meet in the cricket pavilion . . . and that day she came to show us the ring she must have walked up from the Castle to the gate half way up the drive. She leapt over that gate, we were watching at the window . . . (She) went round everybody and showed the engagement ring and stayed quite a while.'

These photographs were taken at Glamis for The People's Journal, *upon her engagement to the Duke of York. The diamond and sapphire ring is clearly visible.*

Elizabeth travelled up to London to her parents' house; they had moved now to 17 Bruton Street. There she found letters, telegrams, photographers and 'gentlemen' of the press awaiting her. Elizabeth wrote to a friend that: 'The cat is completely out of the bag and there is no possibility of stuffing him back'. Somewhat injudiciously she gave an interview to a Mr Cozens-Hardy of *The Star* newspaper. An equerry was sent to Bruton Street to inform Elizabeth that interviews were not to be given, and so her first newspaper interview was also her last. This minor indiscretion aside, Elizabeth was warmly received by the King and Queen. Queen Mary wrote in her journal, 'Elizabeth is with us now, so well brought up, a great addition to the family.'

Life suddenly became very busy for Elizabeth and Bertie. The wedding was set for April 26th, and, as with any wedding, there was an awful lot to be done before then. In March the young couple travelled to Edinburgh to view their wedding cake, a staggering nine feet tall, at the bakery of McVitie & Price; and in the afternoon they attended the Scotland–England rugby match at Murrayfield which England won. The Royal wedding was eagerly anticipated throughout the

Elizabeth, seated at her desk at 17 Bruton Street, having given her first, and last, newspaper interview.

Elizabeth and Bertie visit the McVitie & Price bakery in Edinburgh to view their wedding cake.

Elizabeth is presented with a wedding gift, a silver pen and ink stand, from her own 1st Glamis and Eassie Girl Guides.

country. Presents poured in from all around the world for the young couple. Elizabeth's Glamis Girl Guides presented her with a silver pen and ink stand. The people of Forfar wrote to Elizabeth inquiring as to what might be an appropriate gift. Lady Elizabeth asked her father to reply that she wished no money to be spent. She was well aware that for many people the twenties was a time when 'everyone is feeling the pinch' and, therefore, accepted an illuminated address from the county.

Nonetheless, Elizabeth did receive many beautiful gifts. From her father, a diamond tiara and a necklace of pearls and diamonds, and from Queen Mary, a diamond and sapphire necklace. The King gave her a tiara and complete ensemble of diamonds and turquoises. Bertie chose a necklace of diamonds and pearls, with a pendant to match. She in turn gave Prince Albert a dress watch chain of platinum and pearls.

Elizabeth was the first 'commoner' to marry a Royal Prince for several hundred years, and the public felt closer to her because of this. Her experiences during the war made her wise beyond her years and her ability to get on with people from all walks of life was as prevalent then as it is today. Bertie, too, stepped out from the Royal Ivory Tower. He set up 'The Duke's Camp' where public schoolboys and factory boys holidayed together, so that each could learn from the other. He showed great interest in industrial relations and it was for such efforts that the press had dubbed him 'The Industrial Prince'. Just prior to the wedding, he paid a visit to a trade union, the first member of the Royal family ever to do so. Mr Brownlie, of the Amalgamated Engineering Workers Union, invited the Duke into his office and proposed a toast: 'May the step you are about to take be the happiest of your life and may it continue so. Take my assurance that you are perfectly safe in the hands of a Scots lassie.'

Elizabeth, as the youngest daughter, was especially close to her mother, the Countess of Strathmore.

The Duke was dubbed 'the Industrial Prince' for his interest in the working classes. He is seen here at one of his first camps, at New Romney, 1924.

The Duke and Duchess of York perform their marriage vows before the Archbishop of Canterbury, watched by family and friends inside Westminster Abbey.

The newly weds leave Westminster Abbey for Buckingham Palace.

The morning of April 26th, 1923, Elizabeth left Bruton Street on her father's arm, and travelled by state landau to Westminster Abbey. Her dress was a simple mediaeval style, fashioned from machine made Nottingham lace (to help boost the then flagging lace industry), with a veil of Flanders lace lent to her by Queen Mary. On entering the Abbey, Elizabeth paused and placed her bouquet of York roses and white heather upon the Tomb of the Unknown Soldier. The Duke, wearing the uniform of a Group Captain of the Royal Air Force, waited at the altar. Albert was the first King's son to be married at Westminster Abbey since 1382, when Richard II married Anne of Bohemia, the Chapel Royal having been preferred in later ceremonies.

An official wedding portrait of the Duke and Duchess of York with their parents; King George V and Queen Mary, and the Earl and Countess of Strathmore.

The Archbishop of Canterbury, the Most Reverend Randall Davidson, proceeded with the marriage service, and the Archbishop of York, the Most Reverend Cosmo Gordon Lang, followed with this address:

> You, dear bride, in your Scottish home, have grown up from childhood among countryfolk and friendship with them has been your native air. So have you both been fitted for your place in the people's life, and your separate lives are now, till death, made one. The nations and classes which make up our Commonwealth too often live their lives apart . . . the warm and generous heart of this people takes you today into itself. Will you not in response take that heart, with all its joys and sorrows, into your own?

The Duke and Duchess of York acknowledge the cheers of the crowd as they leave Buckingham Palace to begin their new life together.

Dr Lang was, at that time, the Primus of the Episcopal Church of Scotland, the Church to which Elizabeth belonged. *The Times* issued this comment on the wedding day:

> All its [The Empire] peoples congratulate them on their happiness, and all rejoice with the King and Queen, whose home life has been itself so greatly blessed, in the happiness of their son and of the new daughter he brings them. There is but one wedding to which they look forward with still deeper interest - the wedding which will give a wife to the heir to the throne, and, in the course of nature, a future Queen to England and to the British peoples.

The Smiling Duchess

On honeymoon at Polesden Lacey, the home of Mrs Ronnie Greville.

The Duke and Duchess spent the first part of their honeymoon at Polesden Lacey in Surrey, a beautiful home lent to them by their friend The Hon. Mrs Ronnie Greville. Later they travelled to Glamis where the weather was atrocious and Elizabeth had the misfortune to catch whooping cough, which she later described as 'not a very romantic disease'. The three rooms prepared for them at Glamis served as their private suite whenever they chose to visit the castle, and the rooms are now viewed by the thousands of summer visitors who tour Glamis Castle each year.

The Duke and Duchess arrive at Glamis station to continue their honeymoon. The weather was atrocious and the Duchess caught whooping cough.

Queen Mary with Prince George and the Duke and Duchess of York at Balmoral.

The Duke and Duchess attend an air pageant at Hendon in June 1923. This was their first public engagement together after their wedding.

Elizabeth   26.4.23.   Bertie

Upon return to London the newlyweds found a tremendous number
of public duties and engagements ahead of them. They moved into their
first home of White Lodge in Richmond Park, formerly the home of
Queen Mary, now the home of the Royal Ballet School. Large, draughty
and damp, it was not an ideal house to live in. Unfortunately over the
next year Elizabeth suffered from ill health and after a particularly nasty
bout of bronchitis a holiday was suggested. A trip to East Africa was
arranged for Christmas 1924. The couple went 'on safari'; the Duke big
game hunting, the Duchess preferring to 'shoot' with a camera. They
slept under canvas on the African Plains, and cruised down the Nile by
steamer. The trip lasted four months, and the Yorks were offered their
own farm which they reluctantly had to refuse. They both returned to
Great Britain rested and healthy, and very much in love. In August they
left for Glamis and Balmoral and the Duchess announced that she was
expecting their first child.

The Duke and Duchess pay a visit to Dundee.

With Lord Strathmore at a Glamis Garden Party, c1924.

Princess Elizabeth Alexandra Mary was born at 17 Bruton Street at 2.40 a.m. on April 21st, 1926. *The Times* reported that the 'infant princess' was third in succession to the throne, ranking after her father and the Prince of Wales. The Duke of York responded to a telegram from the Lord Mayor of London saying 'The Duchess and baby are making excellent progress.' After a visit to Bruton Street to see her first grandchild in the male line Queen Mary noted that the new princess was 'a little darling with a lovely complexion and fair hair'. The christening took place in the private chapel at Buckingham Palace on May 29th before a small gathering of family and friends. Princess Elizabeth, wearing a Honiton lace christening robe (first made for Prince Edward VII and worn at every royal christening since) was blessed with Holy Water from the River Jordan; 'Of course poor baby cried', Queen Mary wrote in her diary.

The Yorks planned to settle down to family life when King George V announced that they were to represent him on a World Tour, commencing the following January. They were to open the new Federal Parliament of Australia in Canberra in May, visiting New Zealand, the West Indies, Panama, Polynesia, Mauritius, Malta and Gibraltar along the way. The 'infant princess', only nine months old, was to stay behind with her grandmother, Queen Mary. The Duchess had employed her own nanny, Clara Knight, known to all as Allah, to care for the Princess Elizabeth. But knowing that the ever capable Allah was in charge only partly alleviated her distress at leaving the baby Elizabeth behind. She wrote to Queen Mary of their parting, 'The baby was so sweet playing with the buttons on Bertie's uniform that it quite broke me up.' Sixty years later the present Duchess of York, Sarah, made the same agonising decision, again on Royal Tour to Australia.

The Duke and Duchess set sail aboard the Royal Naval vessel HMS *Renown*, a battle cruiser of 32,000 tons, arriving in New Zealand twenty-two days later. The Duke, who was handicapped by a stutter, had been receiving treatment from Lionel Logue, an Australian speech therapist, in preparation for the tour. His breathing technique assisted the Duke greatly, and it was here in New Zealand that it was first put to the test. The Duke of York wrote to his father, 'I had to make three speeches the first morning . . . I had perfect confidence in myself and I did not hesitate at all. Logue's teaching is still working well, but of course if I get tired it still worries me.'

When Elizabeth fell ill with tonsilitis during the early part of the tour she insisted that he continue on without her, and he was truly surprised at the welcome that the New Zealanders gave him wherever he went. The Duchess rejoined him for the journey to Australia by which time his confidence had been boosted and the prospect of speeches to come

During some precious time off from their World Tour the Duchess relaxes with a spot of fishing in New Zealand.

The Royal couple enjoy a game of quoits with the Hon Mrs Gilmour and Major Nugent aboard HMS *Renown en route to Australia and New Zealand.*

The Duchess's fashions were eagerly anticipated throughout the tour. Here they visited Sydney, on their way to Canberra.

Reunited with Princess Elizabeth at last, after nearly six months away.

seemed a little less daunting. The Australians were thrilled by the Yorks visit; everyone inquired after the baby Princess, and every State enjoyed their presence. As the first Royal lady to visit Australasia for twenty years the Duchess' fashions were eagerly viewed and quickly copied by the society ladies of Auckland and Sydney.

May 7th, 1927, and the day of the Official Opening of Parliament arrived. Although the Duke had gained much confidence throughout his tour the presence of cameras did affect him; however he managed to give a 'perfectly admirable' delivery, and the Duchess, providing encouragement at his side, is reported to have said, 'Darling, how splendid. I am so proud of you!' The Duke was to battle against his impediment throughout his life, but he was ever aided and inspired by his wife.

The tour was considered a resounding success. They had taken Australia and New Zealand by storm. The Governor of South Australia wrote to the King, 'The Duchess has had a tremendous ovation and leaves us with the responsibility of having a continent in love with her.' As the Royal couple sailed out of Sydney harbour aboard HMS Renown to commence the long journey home they were accompanied by various craft. Ignoring the heavy rain they waved farewell to twelve hundred schoolchildren who sang 'Will Ye No Come Back Again' from the deck of a harbour ferry boat. They returned to Portsmouth on June 27th, 1927 and were met by Prince Henry and Prince George and the Prince of Wales. Finally they were reunited with the Princess Elizabeth, who was by now fourteen months old.

The Duchess walks with King George V at a Royal Charity Fête at Balmoral. After the King's death she said; 'I miss him dreadfully. Unlike his own children I was never afraid of him . . . . he was so kind and dependable. And when he was in the mood, he could be deliciously funny too!'

The Duke and Duchess of York visit Glamis with the two year old Princess Elizabeth, in 1928.

The Duke and Duchess open Stirling Royal Infirmary and receive the Freedom of the Burgh in August 1928. The Stirling Journal and Advertiser reported that, 'The Duchess has a happy gift for doing the right thing at the right moment.'

The Yorks moved into their new London home at 145 Piccadilly, and settled down to the family life that they so eagerly sought. However, there is no such thing as a 'normal' life for a member of the Royal family; and they continued to travel throughout the country performing their Royal duties. In 1929 the Duke of York was appointed Lord High Commissioner to the General Assembly of the Church of Scotland, the first Royal for three centuries to be invited to serve. The Duke and Duchess received a tumultuous welcome from the people of Edinburgh as they rode through the streets in an open landau. *The Scotsman* reported: 'The Duke and Duchess had an ovation infused with extraordinary interest and enthusiasm. The association of the King's son and the little Duchess who had become the popular darling of the people transformed the routine of welcome into rapture.'

The Duchess of York gives encouragement to her husband during a speech in Edinburgh, 1929.

Each year they paid a visit to the Strathmore family at Glamis, and it was here that the Duchess of York chose for the birth of her second child, due in August 1930. Princess Margaret Rose was born on a stormy summer night, the first Royal to be born north of the border since 1602. The birth had caused the State considerable inconvenience as it was considered essential that both the Home Secretary and the Ceremonial Secretary be present to witness the birth. The baby was expected to arrive between August 6th and August 12th; however Princess Margaret Rose did not choose to arrive until August 21st. Both men stayed throughout this time with the Dowager Countess of Airlie at Airlie Castle, anxiously waiting for the telephone to ring. One of the first changes that the Duke made after his accession to the throne was to abolish the archaic tradition of witnessing the Royal birth.

Janet Fox recalled the celebrations at Glamis. 'Princess Margaret always said that she was born in a thunderstorm and that was quite right because that day it was terribly hot, so hot the tar was bubbling up on the road and by night time there was a tremendous thunder storm; that was when Princess Margaret was born. We had a bonfire on top of the hill, unfortunately it was wet; however we had dancing around the bonfire, and plenty of kegs of beer for the men. We had quite a time.'

In the drawing room at Glamis Castle on the occasion of the Earl and Countess of Strathmore's Golden Wedding celebrations. Princess Margaret is on her mother's knee, and Princess Elizabeth is seated in the front row with her toy dog.

In 1931 the Yorks visited Glamis again, this time to celebrate the Golden Wedding of the Earl and Countess of Strathmore. A garden party was held in the grounds and all the villagers of Glamis were invited. They presented Lord and Lady Strathmore with wrought iron entrance gates to the castle, a genuinely thoughtful gift which the Earl and Countess greatly appreciated. In 1980 the Queen Mother was presented with similar gates to the Italian Garden at Glamis, a gift from the estate in honour of Her Majesty's eightieth birthday.

King George presented the Yorks with a grace and favour country house, The Royal Lodge in Windsor Park, and this became their family home at weekends. In the grounds was built Y Bwthyn Bach, the little Welsh cottage presented to Princess Elizabeth on her sixth birthday.

Whilst the Duke of Windsor toured extensively overseas the Yorks wanted nothing better than to concentrate on their family life. They made Royal Lodge into their home, and cherished their moments there. Holidays were spent on Deeside and at Glamis, where the Earl and Countess of Strathmore indulged their grandchildren. Glamis possessed

Her Majesty has visited Lord Roberts' Workshops in Dundee every year since her first visit in 1924, excepting two years during the war. The workshops teach woodwork and joinery skills.

The Yorks travelled the length and breadth of the country. They are seen here on the pier at Kyleakin, Isle of Skye, 1933.

Princess Margaret accompanies her mother on a shopping trip to Forfar.

At Glamis station with the Princesses, 1935. On official visits the Duchess always crossed by the bridge, but on less formal occasions she would run across the tracks. Princess Elizabeth is led by her pet corgi 'Dookie'.

all the childhood magic that their mother had enjoyed, and the young princesses loved to visit. They played the popular games of the day, including the rather dangerous practice of placing ha'pennies on the railway tracks, so that the oncoming train could flatten them into pennies. The Duchess was keen for her children to enjoy the same carefree childhood with which she had been blessed; formalities were kept to a minimum and a lot of time was devoted to having fun.

The Queen wished for her own children the same carefree childhood that she had enjoyed. Here the princesses enjoy the Master of Carnegie's 6th birthday party at Elsick House, outside Aberdeen.

In January 1936 King George V, now in his seventy-first year, caught a chill, and his health rapidly deteriorated. On Monday, January 20th, the following official bulletin was released: 'The King's life is moving peacefully towards its close.' At five minutes to midnight the King drew his last breath.

On hearing the news both Houses of Parliament met to take the oath of allegiance to the New King. Clement Attlee, leader of the Opposition gave the following address:

> We offer our loyal service and congratulations to King Edward VIII, who as Prince of Wales has endeared himself to all hearts. He is continuing in a higher sphere and with greater responsibilities the work which he has been doing so well for this country. Like the late King, he showed sympathy with and knowledge of all classes of his subjects, both at home and overseas. He has earned the affection and confidence of all. We know that he will bring to the service of the nation the same great qualities of the mind and heart which his father displayed. May he be spared the same anxieties. The wish of us all is that his reign may be long and prosperous and peaceful.

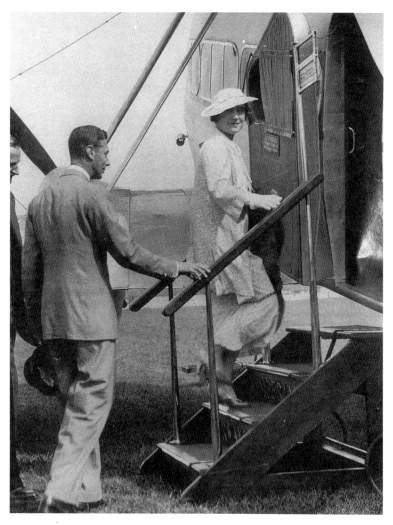

The Duke and Duchess of York fly Imperial Airways to Brussels, the Duchess's first ever air trip. The Duke, an accomplished pilot, was the first member of the Royal family to obtain his wings.

Edward
and
Mrs Simpson

King Edward first met Mr and Mrs Ernest Simpson in November 1930, at a house party held by his friend Mrs Thelma Furness. An American divorcee, Wallis had met and married Englishman Ernest Simpson in London in 1927. In 1931 Mrs Simpson was presented at court, and the Duke of Windsor entertained both Simpsons at his home at Fort Belvedere. In 1935 the Duke went skiing in Kitzbuhl with Mrs Simpson and a group of friends. Ernest Simpson did not join the party.

Upon his accession to the throne it was clear to members of the family that Mrs Simpson was an important part of the King's life. She entertained with him at Fort Belvedere, and, according to Marion Crawford, nanny to the Princesses, she 'appeared to be entirely at her ease, if anything rather too much so.' The King held a dinner in honour of the First Lord Admiral of the Fleet, Sir Samuel Hoare, who commented that Mrs Simpson was 'very attractive and intelligent . . . not only on her sparkling talk, but also her sparkling jewels with up-to-date Cartier settings.'

For the summer holiday the King chartered a yacht, and Mrs Simpson and a group of friends joined him on a cruise of the Dalmatian coast. The Duke and Duchess of York holidayed in Scotland, first to Glamis and then on to Deeside, where the King joined them in September. The King stayed at Balmoral and the Yorks at Birkhall. King Edward had been asked to open Aberdeen Royal Infirmary, of which he had already laid the foundation stone, but because of a build up of work caused by the official period of mourning he declined, and suggested the Duke and Duchess of York in his place. They duly opened the hospital but whilst doing so the King was spotted at Ballater Railway Station awaiting the arrival of Mrs Simpson. In his diaries Sir Henry Channon commented: 'The visit to Balmoral was a calamity, after the King chucked opening the Aberdeen Infirmary, and then openly appeared at Ballater Station on the same day to welcome Wallis to the Highlands. Aberdeen will never forgive him.' The incident was not reported by the British press, which discreetly avoided printing any reference to Mrs Simpson.

The Duke and Duchess of York stand in for the King at the opening of Foresterhill Infirmary in Aberdeen. The King was reported to have met Mrs Simpson at Ballater railway station later that day.

On October 27th Wallis Simpson received her decree nisi and was free to marry. The American press immediately suggested an American Queen Consort for King Edward. The King knew that this was impossible, and therefore suggested a morganatic marriage (a marriage between two persons of unequal rank whose children cannot inherit the higher rank) to the Prime Minister, Stanley Baldwin. This was rejected outright by the self governing countries of the Empire, and the King informed his mother and brothers that he was prepared to abdicate.

American divorcee, Mrs Wallis Simpson, first met the Prince of Wales (later Edward VIII) at a house party in November 1930.

King Edward VIII is refused a morganatic marriage to Mrs Wallis Simpson and makes the momentous decision to abdicate.

Shocked and hurt, Queen Mary wrote to him. 'It seemed inconceivable to those who had made such sacrifice during the war that you, as their King, refused a lesser sacrifice. After all, all my life I have put my country before everything else, and I simply cannot change now.' The King wrote of the Duke of York's reaction in his own memoirs: 'Bertie was so taken aback by my news that in his shy way he could not bring himself to express his innermost feelings at the time. This, after all, was not surprising, for next to myself Bertie had most at stake: it was he who would have to wear the crown if I left, and his genuine concern for me was mixed up with the dread of having to assume the responsibilities of kingship.'

Crowds gather outside the gates of Buckingham Palace as rumours of the Abdication increase.

On December 10th, 1936 the Duke of York witnessed his brother taking the unprecedented step of signing the instrument of Abdication. The document was read in both houses of Parliament the next day. The Prime Minister begged that 'His Majesty's most gracious message be now considered'. The Bill was duly passed. The Archbishop of Canterbury commented : 'If our sympathy goes out to King Edward, it must needs in equal measure go out to the Prince who, in circumstances so sudden and so painful to himself, has been called to take the place of his beloved brother and to face the vast responsibility which he has laid down. We shall surround him and his gracious Consort with a loyalty all the more eager and resolute because it is deepened by our sympathy.'

The Duke of York, travelling to Sandringham for a family Christmas, appears visibly shaken on hearing the news of the Abdication.

INSTRUMENT OF ABDICATION

I, Edward the Eighth, of Great Britain, Ireland, and the British Dominions beyond the Seas, King, Emperor of India, do hereby declare My irrevocable determination to renounce the Throne for Myself and for My descendants, and My desire that effect should be given to this Instrument of Abdication immediately.

In token whereof I have hereunto set My hand this tenth day of December, nineteen hundred and thirty six, in the presence of the witnesses whose signatures are subscribed.

SIGNED AT
FORT BELVEDERE
IN THE PRESENCE
OF

The Instrument of Abdication.

On the evening of Friday December 11th the departing King gave the following speech to the nation:

> At long last I am able to say a few words of my own. I have never wanted to withold anything, but until now it has not been constitutionally possible for me to speak. A few hours ago I discharged my last duty as King and Emperor, and now that I have been succeeded by my brother, the Duke of York, my first words must be to declare my allegiance to him. This I do with all my heart. You all know the reasons which have impelled me to renounce the throne, but I want you to understand that in making up my mind I did not forget the country or the Empire, which as Prince of Wales and lately as King I have for twenty five years tried to serve. But you must believe me when I tell you that I have found it impossible to carry the heavy burden of responsibility and discharge my duties as King as I would wish to do without the help and support of the woman I love . . . This decision has been made less difficult to me by the sure knowledge that my brother, with his long training in the public affairs of this country and with his fine qualities, will be able to take my place forthwith without interruption or injury to the life and progress of the Empire. And he has one matchless blessing, enjoyed by so many of you and not bestowed on me, a happy home with his wife and children . . . And now we all have a new King, I wish him and you, his people, happiness and prosperity with all my heart. God bless you all. God save the King.

The Duke and Duchess of Windsor on honeymoon at Castle Leonburg, June 1937. The coronation of King George VI and Queen Elizabeth had taken place only a month before.

The Queen Consort

The Coronation of Edward VIII had been set for May 12th, 1937. Prime Minister Stanley Baldwin was asked in the House if the date should be postponed, following the Abdication. 'Same day, New King', came his reply.

The Coronation therefore went ahead and on May 12th King George VI was crowned King, with Queen Elizabeth his Consort. He had chosen the name George in a public attempt to emulate his father, George V, who had been such a steadfast and popular monarch. However, in conversation with Mabell, Countess of Airlie, Stanley Baldwin made his views plain. He felt that the new King was beginning his reign with 'a lot of prejudice against him. He's had no chance to capture the popular imagination his brother did. I'm afraid he won't find it easy going for the first year or two.' The press was unsupportive, suggesting that the King's stammer, his lack of 'presence' and his poor academic record at Naval College made him unfit to reign. This was the reaction of a people angered and disappointed by the Abdication, and the new King and Queen knew that they had a difficult task ahead.

The coronation of King George VI and Queen Elizabeth took place on May 12th, 1937.

The Coronation Coach passes by Admiralty Arch on its way to Westminster Abbey.

The Dowager Countess of Airlie was concerned for Elizabeth. 'I pitied most of all the new Queen. In the fourteen years of her marriage she had remained completely unspoiled, still at heart the simple unaffected girl I had known at Glamis, carrying out her public duties with an efficiency that won Queen Mary's admiration but finding her true happiness in her home and her own family circle.' Queen Mary had more confidence. 'The Yorks will do it very well.'

King George V had told the Dowager Countess of Airlie long before his death, 'Bertie has more guts than the rest of his brothers put together.' It was now, in his first reigning year, that his true character was shown to his people. The King accepted his vast responsibility with unrivalled determination. Queen Elizabeth was her husband's source of strength, throughout these difficult times, as always. 'With my wife and helpmeet by my side I take up the heavy task which lies before me,' stated the King in his Accession Speech. And in his first message to Parliament, 'It will be my constant endeavour, with God's help and supported as I shall be by my dear wife, to uphold the Honour of the Realm and promote the

Queen Elizabeth with the young princesses photographed in the garden shortly after their move to Buckingham Palace.

On the eve of the Coronation, crowds of spectators spend a night on the pavements in order to secure a good view of the procession.

happiness of my peoples.' Both King George VI and Queen Elizabeth had felt incredibly moved by the Coronation ceremony. The Duchess of Devonshire commented that 'The Queen is a person of real piety, who felt her crowning acutely.' The Archbishop of Canterbury, Dr Lang, wrote of their service of spiritual preparation. 'After some talk on the spiritual significance of the Coronation, they knelt with me; I prayed for them and for their realm and empire, and I gave them my personal blessing. I was much moved, and so were they. Indeed, there were tears in their eyes when we rose from our knees.' They had pledged themselves

Here the newly crowned King and Queen are seen in Buckingham Palace, with their daughters, in official regalia.

wholeheartedly to the nation, and in doing so they understood that their lives could never be the same again. In his Coronation broadcast George VI announced that 'The Queen and I will always keep in our hearts the inspiration of this day. May we ever be worthy of the goodwill, which, I am proud to think, surrounds us at the outset of my reign. I thank you from my heart, and may God bless you all.' The Coronation over, they began immediately to put their pledge into practice.

The new King and Queen visited Edinburgh in July, and the crowds turned out to cheer them. The Queen was invested with the Order of

Thousands cheered as the new King and Queen stepped onto the balcony at Buckingham Palace.

As the streets of London fill with people in party mood, two spectators ensure a commanding view above the crowds.

Everyone celebrated the Coronation, with street parties and dances throughout the country.

the Thistle at St Giles' Cathedral, the first and only Lady of the Thistle to be appointed. The King surprised his Scottish Queen on the evening of the Coronation, when he presented her with a beautiful diamond badge and star to be worn at her investiture. After the ceremony they travelled to Balmoral for a well earned rest, and here too the people showed their support at Crathie and at the Braemar Gathering. The Queen presented colours to the Black Watch as their newly appointed Colonel-in-Chief, an honour she gladly accepted; three of her brothers had fought with the Black Watch in the last War, Fergus losing his life at the Battle of Loos.

Upon her return to London the Queen was presented with a Doctor of Literature from the University. The degree was a tribute to 'one who fills so nobly the high place to which it has pleased Providence to call her. Scotland has given many good things to England, but none so valued as that daughter who is now our Queen.' By the end of 1937 the grumblings of the press had been forgotten, and King George VI and Queen Elizabeth were firmly established in the hearts of their people.

The crowds turn out at Braemar in 1937 to see the new King and Queen.

World War II

As the New Year commenced it was apparent that a war was brewing in Europe. Hitler's army invaded Austria on March 14th, 1938, and in April he voiced his intent to invade Czechoslovakia. France, as Czechoslovakia's ally, turned to Britain for a promise of support. It was these circumstances which prompted a State Visit to France. The date was set for June 28th, 1938; however the Queen's mother, the Countess of Strathmore, suffered a heart attack on 22nd June. At the age of seventy-five, she had lived through the shock of the Abdication to see her youngest daughter become a respected and loved Queen Consort. Queen Elizabeth, close to her mother as always, rushed to her parent's flat in Portman Square. Lady Strathmore died at 2.00am on June 23rd, 1938, with the King and Queen and her husband and family by her side. The Countess had always practised what she preached. 'Life is for living and working at', she had told the young Lady Elizabeth, and 'If you find anything or anybody a bore the fault is in yourself.' *The Times* obituary stated: 'She possessed a genius for family life - a most rare and priceless gift. She had a great power of loving, an unusual power of sympathy and a rare understanding of other people.' And the Archbishop of

The Queen looks stunning in a Norman Hartnell creation in Paris, 1938. The Queen wore white throughout the tour as a mark of respect to her mother who had died only weeks before.

Canterbury, the Most Reverend Dr Cosmo Gordon Lang said: 'She raised a Queen in her own home, simply, by trust and love and as a return the Queen has won widespread love.'

The funeral took place at Glamis, in the pouring rain. The Royal Couple paid their last respects to a charismatic and dearly loved old lady, then hid their private grief, their duty taking precedence over personal considerations. The Royal Tour went ahead on July 19th, 1938, only three weeks later than the original tour date. The Queen arranged for all her clothes, specially created by Norman Hartnell for the State Visit, to be copied in white, an official colour of mourning, as a mark of respect to her mother.

The Royal Couple departed on July 19th, anxious to cement Anglo-French relations, should they be drawn into the war. The Queen, in her stunning crinolines, 'captured Paris by storm', and the Parisian crowds cheered the Royal Couple wherever they went. Lady Diana Cooper, who travelled on the tour, recalled, 'We saw the King and Queen from a window, coming down the Champs Elysées with roofs, windows and pavements roaring exultantly, the Queen a radiant Winterhalter.'

During the State Visit the King's ministers had long discussions with their French counterparts, and it was agreed that a mission be sent to the Czechs to persuade them to accept some form of compromise with Hitler. This was rejected outright by the Führer, who, rather than invade Czechoslovakia, gave further support to the rebellion of Sudeten Germans within that country. Things were not looking good. On September 22nd Prime Minister Neville Chamberlain flew

The King and Queen return from their triumphant tour of France. Reunited with the princesses they take a well earned rest aboard the Royal yacht Victoria and Albert.

The Royal family in an open Landau on their way to church at Crathie, August 1939.

to Germany to meet with Hitler, to discuss a solution to the 'Czech problem'. He returned to inform the King that war was imminent, and the British Government prepared itself accordingly. Gas masks were issued, trenches were dug, and children were evacuated from London.

The King and Queen were due to visit Clydebank on September 27th, 1938, to launch the world's largest liner, the *Queen Elizabeth*. However, the situation was considered to be so grave that the King felt unable to leave London. Not wishing to disappoint her people the Queen met with the princesses (who had been staying at Balmoral), in Glasgow, and they travelled to Clydebank. As she launched the great ship she told the assembled crowd: 'This ceremony, to which many thousands have looked forward so eagerly, must now take place in circumstances far different from those for which they had hoped, . . . (the King) bids the people of this country to be of good cheer, in spite of the dark clouds hanging over them, and, indeed, over the whole world.'

The Queen launches the Cunard liner, Queen Elizabeth, the most luxurious ship of its time, which immediately stood by for active service and only became a cruise liner when the war was over.

66

Neville Chamberlain returned to Germany and met Hitler with Mussolini and Daladier in Munich. On September 30th he landed at Heston Airport, waving the Anglo-German Agreement he had signed with Hitler and proclaiming 'Peace in Our Time'. On March 10th 1939 Chamberlain stated that 'the outlook in international affairs is tranquil'. On March 15th Hitler proclaimed 'Czechoslovakia has ceased to exist'.

It was decided that the King and Queen should tour Canada and the United States, in an effort to rally support from the Commonwealth and our strongest ally. In Canada the King and Queen were treated with a rapturous reception wherever they went, and they went everywhere. The King insisted on visiting every Province, and the Canadians loved him for it. There was some concern as to how the French Canadians might

The Rocky Mountains provide a spectacular backdrop for the Royal Couple during their tour of the United States and Canada in the summer of 1939. They are seen here with the Canadian Prime Minister, W.L. Mackenzie King.

The Queen chats with a girl scout during their Majesties' tour of the USA.

react to the tour. The Queen gave her speech in French and in English, and the French were appeased. The Governor General of Canada, Lord Tweedsmuir (formerly John Buchan, the novelist) wrote, 'The visit is going to have an enormous effect on Canada and in the United States . . . as a demonstration of our unity of spirit. Our monarchs are most remarkable young people . . . as for the Queen, she has a perfect genius for the right kind of publicity . . . at the unveiling of the War Memorial, where we had some ten thousand veterans, she asked me if it was not possible to get a little closer to them . . . it was an amazing sight, for we were simply swallowed up.'

According to Dorothy Laird, in her book *Queen Elizabeth the Queen Mother*:

> Everywhere they went in Canada they met Scots. The King once remarked, when advised for the umpteenth time that at the train's next halting place a group of people emanating from Kirriemuir would be assembled, that Canada seemed to be entirely peopled by the men of Angus.

At Windsor, on the Canadian/American border, people lined more than five miles of railway track to greet the Royal Couple. Americans poured over the border to join the already waiting Canadians and a crowd estimated at half a million cheered and waved. A member of the Royal party later stated, 'I have never seen such crowds as those in Canada. As we proceeded, they grew and grew. The word of the King and Queen's tremendous success spread ahead of us, so that the build-up was terrific.' Throughout the visit the King and Queen interrupted their official programme to talk to the people who had turned out to see them, establishing the first Royal walkabouts.

The tour of the United States was a further resounding success. The Republican Americans received the King and Queen most warmly. There was some anxiety that the American people may have reacted against the Royal Couple, as it had been popularly felt that Mrs Simpson's nationality had been the reason for the Abdication, however this was not in evidence. In Washington they received a tumultuous reception. A Texan member of the House of Representatives boldly stated, 'Cousin Elizabeth, you're a thousand times more pretty than your pictures.'

In New York they were welcomed by ferries, boats and fire-fighting craft as they sailed into harbour. They visited the Court of Peace, and joined President and Mrs Roosevelt at their country home, Hyde Park. Both the King and Queen were impressed with the Roosevelts, and respect was mutual. 'I admired both of them and found the Queen a warm and positive personality,' wrote America's First Lady. Queen Elizabeth, in her farewell speech, stated, 'This wonderful tour of ours has given me memories that the passage of time will never dim . . . '

Upon their return to Britain in July 1939, the threat of war was becoming a reality. In August the family travelled to Balmoral, and the King held his annual camp at Abergeldy Castle, only a few miles away. The boys, coming from very different backgrounds, mixed well, and the camp was a happy one. However, as the Royal Family joined the campers in a sing song, Germany was preparing to invade Poland. The King returned to London, and was soon followed by the Queen. Within a fortnight Britain was at war, and the young men of the King's camp were joining the Services. The Queen was said to resemble her mother in those early days of the war, 'A tower of strength'. She, in turn, took her strength from her faith. The Strathmore family motto; 'In thou my God, I place my trust without changes to the end' provided comfort, as it had in difficult times past.

The King's camp at Abergeldy, August 1939. The King encouraged public schoolboys and factory boys to holiday together, so that each could learn from the other. However, this group were soon to be in khaki; as they all sing 'Under the spreading chestnut tree' the threat of Nazism spreads even nearer.

At Buckingham Palace staff immediately rejoined their regiments, and a Home Guard was formed amongst those who remained. It was decided that the Princesses should evacuate to Windsor; but the King and Queen steadfastly refused to leave London themselves, even during the Blitz. Early in the war it was suggested that the Princesses be sent to Canada but this was rejected outright by the Queen. 'The Princesses will never leave without me, I will not leave without the King - and the King will never leave.' In his 1939 Christmas broadcast the King shared the following prayer with the nation:

> I said to the man who stood at the gate of the year: give me a light that I may tread safely into the unknown and he replied: go into the darkness and put your hand into the hand of God. That shall be to you better than light and safer than a known way.

The Queen looks the East End in the face in 1940.

During the worst of the bombing, they visited London's East End, to see the destruction and carnage for themselves. The Queen wrote to Queen Mary. 'I feel quite exhausted after seeing and hearing so much sadness, sorrow, heroism and magnificent spirit. The destruction is so awful and the people are so wonderful - they deserve a better world.' When Buckingham Palace was hit, she said, 'I'm glad we've been bombed. It makes me feel I can look the East End in the face.' The Palace was bombed nine times in all, and the Guards Chapel was completely destroyed, killing over a hundred people. But it was not only the East End whom Her Majesty could look in the face. With the King she travelled the length and breadth of Britain by train, inspecting troops and battle stations, factories and farms. Together they visited the homeless and bereaved, providing hope and encouragement with each visit.

Opposite: The King and Queen see the destruction of the Blitz for themselves.

The King and Queen inspect the bomb damage at Buckingham Palace in September 1940.

Visiting a WRVS centre in London, 1940.

The homeless of Sheffield receive a few words of comfort from the King and Queen.

Her Majesty shares a joke with a lance corporal in the Royal Engineers on a midnight stop at Perth railway station.

The Queen gave the following message to the women of Britain.

War has at all times called for the fortitude of women . . . Their lot was all the harder because they felt that they could do so little beyond heartening, through their own courage and devotion, the men at the front. Now this is all changed, for we no less than men have real and vital work to do. To us also is given the proud privilege of serving our country in her hour of need . . . I know that it is not so difficult to do the big things . . . But these things are not for every woman. It is the thousand and one worries and irritations in carrying on wartime life in ordinary homes which are often so hard to bear. Many of you have had to see your family life broken up - your husband going off to his allotted task, your children evacuated to places of greater safety. The King and I know what it means to be parted from our children, and we can sympathise with those of you who have bravely consented to this separation for the sake of your little ones . . .

The Queen pays a visit to aircraft workers making equipment for the RAF.

The Queen sees for herself conditions in a London bomb shelter.

Whilst the menfolk were overseas serving King and Country, the women of Britain were, quite literally 'keeping the home fires burning'. In an address to the Women's Institute in the Royal Albert Hall the Queen spoke the following words.

> Today our villages are sadly empty, the young men are away fighting for the land they love so well, and the girls, too, are away on their war work. The great responsibility of carrying on rests with older women, and how gallantly they are doing this, shouldering every sort of job with a grand and cheerful spirit. Today the place of the countrywoman is more important than it has ever been before. Despite all the wartime difficulties, it is she who must care for the workers who are growing our food, use her skill to make the most of that food, bring up her children to love and defend those values for which we are fighting, and guide them to love and cherish the beautiful country of which we are so proud.

The King and Queen chat to Aberdeen trawlermen on a visit to the harbour in 1940.

The Queen listens to an ARP warden during
her visit to Glasgow.

Caledon Shipyard, Dundee, 1941. Royal visits did
much to boost morale during the War.

Visit to Southern Command, July, 1941.

On August 25th, 1942, the Duke of Kent left Balmoral Castle, where he had been spending a few days with the King and Queen, to fly to Iceland where he was due to inspect RAF bases. His plane crashed in the Scottish mountains, and he was killed. The King, who had been very fond of his younger brother, felt his loss most keenly.

Buckingham palace was rationed, just as the rest of Britain. An American newspaper reporter asked the Queen if she had ever tasted Woolton Pie, a Ministry of Food concoction comprising of carrots, parsnips, turnips and potatoes with white sauce and pastry. She replied,

The Queen's ability to keep cheerful throughout the War was an inspiration to many.

'Yes, I have. Have you?' When Eleanor Roosevelt visited in 1942, she recorded 'We were served on gold and silver plates, but our bread was the same kind of war bread every other family had to eat . . . nothing was ever served that was not served in any war canteen.'

The Royal Family was anxious for the people of Britain to see that they contributed to the War Effort in a personal way. The Queen and her staff made bandages and dressings for the Red Cross, whilst the King spent two evenings a week making ammunition. Towards the end of the war, Princess Elizabeth joined the ATS and became a second subaltern in the motor transport section.

On November 7th, 1944, the Queen's father, Lord Strathmore, having been unwell for some time, died at Glamis at the age of eighty-nine. The King and Queen were accompanied on the long walk to the family burial ground by pipers of the Black Watch, who played the haunting air *Flowers o' the Forest* as the Earl was laid to rest. His death was followed by that of President Roosevelt in April 1945. The bond between the Roosevelts and the Royal Couple had been cemented on their Royal tour to the United States in 1939. Their friendship paved the way for the special Anglo-American relationship that exists to this day. The loss of President Roosevelt was felt on both sides of the Atlantic.

The Queen joins members of her household in the Blue Drawing Room at Buckingham Palace to make dressings and clothes for the Red Cross.

The unconditional surrender of Germany was announced on May 8th, 1945 and the war in Europe was over. Crowds gathered outside Buckingham Palace, calling for the King and Queen. They were not to be disappointed. Their Majesties, accompanied by the Princesses Elizabeth and Margaret, and Prime Minister Winston Churchill, waved to the crowds from the bomb damaged balcony. On August 15th, 1945, the Japanese surrendered after the destruction of Hiroshima and Nagasaki by atom bomb. The Second World War was finally over. The King and Queen again responded to the crowds and came onto the balcony. On this occasion Princess Elizabeth and Princess Margaret joined the crowd outside the gates to the Palace and cheered their parents as noisily as those surrounding them.

Victory in Europe. Prime Minister, Winston Churchill, joins the Royal Family on the balcony at Buckingham Palace as they acknowledge the cheers from the crowd.

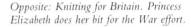

Opposite: Knitting for Britain. Princess Elizabeth does her bit for the War effort.

The War is over and everyone is looking forward to building a new Britain. The Queen, on the Scottish Tour of 1946, smiles at baby Frank Quinn, one of the new generation.

79

The war over, the King knew that the next few years would be difficult for Britain. 'Make no mistake, there is a very hard time waiting for us after the war. The killing will have stopped, but our troubles will be great.' Rationing was still in force, and was to continue until 1954.

For the King and Queen, as for so many people, the war had changed their lives irrevocably. According to the Queen's brother, Sir David Bowes Lyon, 'It was when the war was over that the King and Queen realised that they could never go back to a secluded life.'

Whilst touring the Scottish Borders the King accepts a red rose, traditionally presented to the Sovereign when passing through the area.

Peace at
Last

Princess Elizabeth married her childhood sweetheart, Prince Philip of Greece and Denmark on November 20th, 1947. It was the first great State occasion since the war, and it seemed that everyone wanted to enjoy themselves. According to *Country Life*: 'The crowd was enormous, nothing like it had been seen in London since the Coronation ten years ago. And it was a happy, good tempered crowd obviously determined to enjoy its brief escape from what we have come to call austerity. Flags and streamers flowered from every other hand, and countless periscopes . . . danced like crystallised sunshine above the tightly packed heads.' The King wrote to his newly married daughter, 'I was so proud of you and thrilled at having you so close to me on our long walk in Westminster Abbey, but when I handed your hand to the Archbishop I felt that I had lost something very precious': a sentiment shared by many fathers on their daughter's wedding day.

The following year the King and Queen celebrated their silver wedding anniversary and the Queen broadcast this heartfelt message to the nation:

> Looking back over the last twenty-five years and to my own happy childhood, I realise more and more the wonderful sense of security and happiness that comes from a loved home. Therefore at this time my heart goes out to all those who are living in uncongenial surroundings and who are longing for the time when they will have a home of their own.

Princess Elizabeth and the Duke of Edinburgh are joined by the King and Queen, Queen Mary, Princess Margaret and bridesmaids on the balcony at Buckingham Palace, after their wedding at Westminster Abbey in November 1947.

The King and Queen celebrate twenty five years of marriage.

The Queen accepts a shepherd's crook from the Braemar Royal Highland Society.

In November there was further joy as they celebrated the birth of their first grandchild, Prince Charles. However, their happiness was masked by the King's illness and the serious news that he was in danger of losing his right leg. Despite her own anxiety, the Queen took the King's place at official engagements; determined to 'carry on', come what may. The King underwent a successful operation, but was told that he must rest.

The Royal family arrives at Ballater station for the annual holiday at Balmoral, 1948.

The Queen with her first grandchild, Prince Charles.

On the Queen's fiftieth birthday *The Times* wrote:

> It would be impossible to over-estimate the reinforcement that the King has derived from the serene and steady support of the Queen. She has sustained him in sickness and in health, at all times taking her full share in the burdens of royal service and in the time of great anxiety that befell her during the King's grave illness, piling new duties upon her already overcrowded programme in order that no good cause that had been promised the encouragements of royal patronage might be avoidably disappointed. She speaks to all men and women on the level of common experience . . . She is never afraid to challenge the over-sophisticated of the age in which she lives; she ignores the cynics and the pessimists and holds up for admiration the things that are lovely and of good report. She would commend to all what she told the University of Cape Town were the four cardinal virtues of academic life: honesty, courage, justice and resolve, the whole sustained upon the simplicities and the profundities of faith. These simple virtues have provided the tenets by which Her Majesty has chosen to live, and they have provided a clear path for those who have chosen to follow her example.

The King with his family at Balmoral. This was to be his last holiday on Deeside.

The Queen out walking on the Balmoral estate with her daughters. Following behind Princess Margaret is Group Captain Peter Townsend.

Princess Elizabeth took on many of her father's daily tasks, helped throughout by her mother. In August 1951, the whole family travelled to Balmoral, the King and Queen, Princess Elizabeth and the Duke of Edinburgh with their children Prince Charles and Princess Anne, and Princess Margaret. They celebrated Princess Margaret's twenty-first birthday, but all the family knew that the King was not well. It was to be his last happy holiday on Deeside.

Princess Elizabeth and the Duke of Edinburgh decided to undertake the King and Queen's postponed tour to Australia and New Zealand.

The King and Queen with their grandchildren, Prince Charles and Princess Anne.

As the King's health failed, family outings to the theatre became less frequent.

The evening prior to their departure the whole family enjoyed an evening at the Theatre Royal, Drury Lane, where they watched the premiere performance of the musical *South Pacific*. The following day, January 31st, 1952, the King waved his daughter off on the first leg of her journey to Kenya. Six days later he died peacefully in his sleep, at Sandringham. At the age of fifty-one, Queen Elizabeth was a widow.

The King's coffin, bearing the Imperial Crown and the Queen Mother's wreath, is carried into Westminster Hall for the official lying in state.

The Queen Mother, accompanied by the Queen, Princess Margaret and Queen Mary, await the arrival of the King's body at Westminster Hall.

Clement Attlee, in his appreciation of King George, wrote, 'happy in his marriage, and in his family life . . . in all his work he had the help and support of the gracious lady who was an ideal Consort. As Queen and wife and mother she won a firm place in the hearts of the people.' Lady Elphinstone spoke of their marriage, 'They were so particularly together; they both leaned so much on the other. It was Queen Elizabeth's gift to be able to encourage and reward the King with a look or a smile.' And Winston Churchill said, in his farewell salute:

> For fifteen years King George the Sixth was King. Never at any moment in all the perplexities at home and abroad, in public and private, did he fail in his duties. Well does he deserve this farewell salute of all his governments and peoples.

> My friends, it is at this time that our compassion and sympathy go out to his Consort and widow. Their marriage was a love match with no idea of regal pomp or splendour. Indeed there seemed to be before them the arduous life of royal personages,

denied so many of the activities of ordinary folk and having to give so much in ceremonial public service.

May I say, speaking with all freedom, that our hearts go out tonight, to that valiant woman with famous blood of Scotland in her veins, who sustained King George through all his toils and problems, and brought up, with their charm and beauty the two daughters who mourn their father today. May she be granted strength to bear her sorrow.

As the Queen Mother came to terms with her private sorrow, twenty thousand people queued quietly each day along the Thames Embankment to Westminster to pay their last respects to their King.

Over twenty thousand people queue along the embankment to pay their last respects to the King.

The Queen Mother

Her Majesty Queen Elizabeth the Queen Mother performs her first official function after the death of her husband. She inspects the troops of the 1st Battalion Black Watch and wishes them Godspeed as they set sail for Korea in May 1952.

The Queen Mother could have chosen to retire from public life, but her strong sense of duty, her overwhelming desire not to disappoint, brought her back into public view. Upon the King's death Her Majesty spoke of their shared purpose: 'Throughout our married life we have tried, the King and I, to fulfil with all our hearts and all our strength the great task of service that was laid upon us. My only wish now is to continue the work that we sought to do together.'

The 1st Battalion of the Black Watch was ordered to serve in Korea in May 1952. As their Colonel-in-Chief she had always wished her Regiment 'God speed' before going on active service. This occasion was to be no different. Her Majesty travelled to Crail, to the delight of her soldiers, who each wore a black armband as a mark of respect to the late King. In her speech to the men she said:

> The Black Watch, so dear to my heart and to many of my family who have served with the Regiment, has for more than two hundred years played a distinguished part in the battles of our Country. I am proud to think that the traditions which have made you great are cherished and upheld today and I know well that whatever may face you, you will win new honour for the Black Watch and for Scotland.

As she watched the Coronation of Queen Elizabeth II from the Royal gallery in Westminster Abbey, Her Majesty must have felt a tremendous pride in her daughter, who, from the age of ten, had been trained to fulfil the role of Monarch. The stability and tremendous popularity of the monarchy at the time of Queen Elizabeth II's Coronation was entirely due to the fifteen years of hard work, dedication and loyalty that King George VI and Queen Elizabeth had selflessly given to their people. The new Queen knew that she too would have to give that same wholehearted dedication to duty.

The Queen Mother, with Prince Charles and Princess Margaret, watch the coronation of Queen Elizabeth II from the Royal box.

For Prince Charles the ceremony seemed to go on and on . . .

'It is too common an experience to find that once a house becomes deserted, its decay begins. It is a happiness to me to feel that I have been able to save from such an unworthy fate part of Scotland's heritage. It is a delight to me that I now have a home in Caithness.' The Queen Mother talking about the Castle of Mey.

It was whilst holidaying in Caithness with her friends Commander and Lady Doris Vyner that the Queen Mother first set eyes on Barrogill Castle. Left to rot, it was almost a ruin and was due for demolition. She made enquiries and purchased the castle and, whilst restoring its fabric, she restored its name, The Castle of Mey.

One of the builders involved in the restoration recalled that the Queen Mother was concerned with even the finest of details, particularly when it came to interior decoration and colour schemes. She frequently called at the Castle to see how work was progressing. On one particular occasion an apprentice's overalls were dirty and so the foreman hid the boy in a

The Queen Mother greets her family as they step ashore at Dwarick pier to pay their first visit to the Castle of Mey.

94

Her Majesty found the informal friendly atmosphere of Caithness a refreshing tonic.

cupboard. The Queen Mother chose to open that very cupboard and was highly amused by the incident.

In 1955 the Royal Yacht *Britannia* sailed as near to the Castle as it dared (the Castle overlooks the treacherous Pentland Firth) and the Royal Family came ashore by launch to visit Her Majesty in her new home. Each year they have continued to visit; however the Royal Yacht now makes for the safer waters of Scrabster harbour. In Caithness the Queen Mother found the quiet solitude that she had been seeking; she could walk along the sands, go shopping in Thurso, visit the church at Canisbay and nobody would bother her. Upon receiving the Freedom of Wick in 1956, she said:

> When, on one of my first visits three or four years ago, I found the Castle of Mey with its long history, its serene beauty, and its proud setting, faced with the prospect of having no-one able to occupy it I felt a great wish to preserve, if I could, this ancient dwelling. It is too common an experience to find that once a house becomes deserted, its decay begins. It is a happiness to me that I have been able to save from such an unworthy fate part of Scotland's heritage. It is such a delight to me that I now have a home in Caithness, a county of such great beauty, compiling, as it does, the peace and tranquility of an open and uncrowded countryside with the rugged glory of a magnificent coastline, a remote attachment of country villages, with the busy and independent life of the market towns. I feel at home.

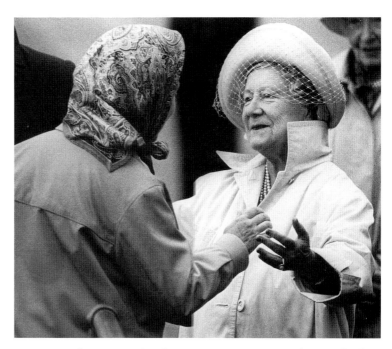

The Queen Mother greets the Queen as she steps ashore at Scrabster, Caithness.

The Queen Mother visits Caithness every august and attends the annual Mey Games. This is always a relaxed affair, a mixture of locals and tourists alike, all 'mucking in' and having fun. The Tug-of-War is always the highlight and Her Majesty presents the prize to the winning team. On her farm at Long Goe she keeps her herd of Aberdeen Angus cattle and her flock of North Country cheviot sheep.

The garden at Mey is a particular source of pride. What was once derelict land next to the Castle is now a pretty rose garden, with a

The Queen Mother with her herd of Aberdeen Angus cattle on her farm at Mey.

The Mey games held every August, is a friendly, informal affair.

path of shells taken from the beach. Sheltered under the Castle wall is a fruit and vegetable garden and hardier plants and flowers are nurtured lovingly; the harsh Caithness wind blowing away any striplings. The Queen Mother's love for gardens and gardening stems from her mother, who designed the Italian Garden at Glamis. On a sunny day, she likes nothing better than to sit in her rose garden, enjoying the sea air.

Every year the Queen Mother visits the art exhibition in Thurso Town Hall, arranged by the Society of Caithness Artists. In honour of Her Majesty's eightieth birthday the Society decided to give the Queen

The Queen Mother, accompanied by her dogs, enjoys the sunshine in her garden at the Castle of Mey.

Her Majesty visits the Caithness Artists' Exhibition every year, and knows many of the artists personally.

97

Mey is where the Queen Mother goes to get away from it all. Her Majesty stands at the rear entrance to the Castle with the Pentland Firth behind her.

Mother a unique present – seven miniature paintings of her favourite views of Caithness. To celebrate the birthday the Caithness folk treated Her Majesty to a ceilidh at the Castle of Mey. She was entertained by the champion piper in Scotland, the champion traditional singer in Scotland, and the champion mouth organist in Scotland, all of whom lived in Caithness. Miss Henrietta Munro recalled: 'I think she enjoyed that very much, and that was something that nobody else could give her.'

Opposite page: Her Majesty dancing the Dashing White Sergeant with Sgt Major Alan Ferrier of the Territorial Army at the Jubilee Ball, Assembly Rooms, Wick, in 1977.

Her Majesty at the launching of Thurso's new lifeboat, August 1989.

The Queen Mother's fishing hut on the River Dee was a present from her family for her 80th birthday.

The Queen Mother fishes on the River Thurso and on the River Dee. In 1980 her family had a fishing hut specially built for her on Deeside as a birthday surprise. Her ghillie of many years, now retired, considers Her Majesty to be an expert fly fisherman; she has that essential quality needed to catch fish – patience.

When visiting Deeside the Queen Mother stays at Birkhall, 'next door' to Balmoral Castle, on the banks of the River Dee. She attends the

Birkhall is the Queen Mother's residence on Deeside.

The Royal family enjoys the sports at the Braemar Gathering, 1971.

With her grandchildren Prince Charles, Lady Sarah Armstrong-Jones and Viscount Linley at Crathie, 1969.

Braemar Gathering each year and has been joined in recent years by the younger members of the Royal Family, The Prince and Princess of Wales and The Duke and Duchess of York. Her keen sense of family and duty to the home has been rewarded with the blessing of great-grandchildren. Peter and Zara Phillips were soon followed by Prince William and Prince Henry; then came Princess Beatrice, and most recently, Princess Eugenie.

The Royal family enjoys a joke at Braemar in September 1989.

The Queen Mother has attended the Braemar Gathering every year since 1923.

The Royal family watches the Trooping of the Colour from the balcony at Buckingham Palace.

Pictured at Glamis with her great-grandnephews, The Queen Mother cradles the Hon. John Fergus Bowes Lyon, accompanied by Simon Patrick, Lord Glamis, heir to the Strathmore title.

She sustains, and is sustained by her own large and happy family, whom she loves unconditionally and of which she is the central figure. In a birthday address the Archbishop of Canterbury, Dr Robert Runcie, described Her Majesty's love of her people: 'What we have seen in one greatly loved and universally admired lady is a love which has been given through her to us, and returned to her by us, and then given out again by her. Over and over again.'

Her Majesty on the occasion of her eighty-second birthday is surprised with a cake from the cast of The Pirates of Penzance *at the Theatre Royal, Drury Lane.*

The Queen Mother, surrounded by her family, at the wedding of her third grandchild, Prince Andrew to Sarah Ferguson.

The Queen Mother looks on proudly at the christening of Prince William, her third great grandchild.

In Scotland, it seems that we have always known and loved her. Since her teenage years at Glamis she has served her people, of whom she has an innate understanding. Although born in London, Her Majesty has frequently alluded to her Scots ancestry. On tour in South Africa in 1947 she met an old Afrikaner who, although pleased to meet the Royal Family, made it clear that he did not like being governed by Westminster. 'I understand perfectly. We feel the same in Scotland,' came the reply. In the words of her late friend, Miss Henrietta Munro, 'She has a great love

The Queen Mother, as First Chancellor of Dundee University, chats with students after the opening ceremony.

Prince Charles accompanies the Queen Mother to the Order of the Thistle ceremony in Edinburgh. The order was first conferred upon her by George VI in 1937.

of all things Scottish, well, after all, she *is* Scottish.' Even the diehard republican Willie Hamilton, retired M.P. for Central Fife, (who lists his recreation in *Who's Who* as 'attacking monarchy'), can't help but melt before Her Majesty. In an eightieth birthday address he wrote ' . . . my hatchet is buried. My venom dissipated. I am glad to salute a remarkable old lady. Long may she live to be the pride of her family. And may God understand and forgive me if I have been ensnared and corrupted, if only briefly, by this superb Royal trouper.'

An 80th birthday portrait of the Queen Mother with her two daughters taken by Norman Parkinson.

The Queen Mother celebrates her 80th birthday with the Queen and Prince Philip and Princess Margaret at Holyrood House.

Balmoral Castle.

In 1986, as the Queen Mother dined with her family at Balmoral, a fishbone became lodged in her throat. She was rushed to Aberdeen Royal Infirmary, the hospital that she and her husband had opened fifty years before. Thankfully the bone was removed. Her Majesty travelled to Caithness to continue her holiday, apparently unperturbed, and the world gave a heartfelt sigh of relief.

With 1st Battalion, 51st Highland Volunteers at Perth in 1986.

Whether young or old, the Queen Mother gets on with everyone.

The Queen Mother visits her beloved city of Dundee, accompanied by Mary, Countess of Strathmore.

As Her Majesty approaches her ninetieth birthday and tributes pour in from all over the Commonwealth and throughout the world, we in Scotland salute her and thank her for her lifelong service to her people. She continues to carry out her considerable duties with the freshness and vitality of a woman half her age and always with that famous smile. Her continual zest for life and her interest in everyone and everything around her, is an inspiration to us all.

Her Majesty opens the new Drama College at the Royal Scottish Academy of Music and Drama.

The Queen Mother seems unable to retire. On a gruelling tour of Canada she waves to crowds, accompanied by Royal Mounties.